dance on a dirt road

POEMS FOR LIFE'S ROUGH PLACES

NANCY CALHOUN

To Betty,
with pleasure
in the writing!

Nancy Calhoun

ISBN: 1453893555
ISBN-13: 9781453893555

For

Linda, Laura, David and Scott
and all who have come after...

by far my best work

Everyone has rough places in their lives. This is a book that celebrates the highs and lows of being alive, and how the silken thread of poetry has helped me to hear my own voice and find my way through it all. I am supported and loved by the most wonderful family and a myriad of dear friends, whose faith in me never waivers, for which I am profoundly grateful. I would especially like to thank Scott Stewart, whose collaboration on this book means the world to me.

I hope that something here speaks to you.

— Nancy Calhoun

CONTENTS

Hope

Home

Healing

We rarely hear the inward music, but we're all dancing to it, nevertheless.

— Rumi

HOPE

....

Dance on a Dirt Road

In the hushed hour, she emerges from her cocoon
one limb at a time, eases through the cobweb casing
to step into the afterlife of the full moon.
She feels erotic, naked, though she wears a silken gown
the color of spring leaves and pearls of dew.
A syncopated wind slips over her skin
as she begins to dance, one with sky and earth.

Curls of red dust swirl upward as her feet lift
and twirl, hesitant at first, then fleet and swift,
taking no notice of rocks and ruts, feeling light,
free of her perilous existence, perfect in body,
sinuous with longing, transformed in the lunar glow.
She is fire, wind and luminosity, propelled
on a zephyr, wild with power, creating God.

Nightbirds call in the quiet chaos left by her shadow.
From her hands she unleashes ribbons braided
of fears and failures, laced with heart fragments.
She spins tenaciously, arms spread like wings and dances
for all she has missed in her lonely space.
This road knows her feet, feels the beat she hears
in her head, a concerto for a lone dancer, with grace.

Star Light

the weight of all those wishes upon the first star
must be difficult to bear, the whole planet
thrumming with desires, mourning broken dreams,
longing to end their longing, to once again
surge with hunger for the life they intended.

star bright, just one small wish is all they ask.
right my boat, let me sail smooth seas, let me float
far from here where I have lost the memories,
lost the answers, the compass —
set me a new course, dear star, set me free.

in the early twilight I see it, a gleaming pearl
alone in the dusky violet, as though it shines
on only me, and I send up a quiet yearning,
keep this small boat on this small sea
headed toward hope.

Early Walk

Before six in the cool morning
I walk my red dirt road
for the miracle of daily gratitude.

Rose-hued mountains encircle,
a slight chill ensuring
I am fully awake in the dappled light.

It is quiet but not silent.
Roosters swagger the dawn,
dogs alert to my presence.

A quail family panics in a thrumping
outburst of fragile wings, lifting together,
like my heart in praise of small things.

At a curve up a small grade, sun behind her
like a halo, a doe stands motionless.
We bless each other without a sound.

She thrusts herself forward
in so light a leap that she is gone
with only an elegant flicker of white.

I turn for home, seized with love,
my generous miracle gratefully
accepted and absolute.

Diagnosis

The sun rose again this morning, as predicted,
unaware of how different, how gravely unlike
today is from yesterday,

how I feel as though I have been suddenly stranded
in a foreign land with no creased and folded map
to find my way back to familiar surroundings.

It is just a word, yet I can only sigh and stare
from my window, where the abundant plants
and stony foothills remain as they were

before I knew the word, before my body
had assailed me, like being left by a lover
without whom you can't breathe.

I keep my fear braided tightly, too soon
to come apart, I tell myself, there will be time
later to strew my quiet wreckage about.

The sun will rise again tomorrow, I suppose,
and won't bother to check on my condition,
if I need anything, if my breath has returned

to normal, if indeed *anything* can be normal.
I look out at the mountains, my eyes grown
hungry, not wanting to turn away.

I want to wrap the sunrise within the folds
of my robe, to feel its heat like a knife in the space
between my ribs, to pierce the dread of the future.

Panic is a handful of smoke, and I am weary
of pursuing the unattainable. I bend into
the moment, the precious present, and the irony

of uncertainty upon which we all feast, inviting
life to give us all we desire, and none of what we
fear. I carry one word into the day...nevertheless.

Until further notice...

so this is how it will be,
not what I would have chosen,
to be sure, but until further notice

the music will continue, all the more
lively and boisterous, the songs rich
as ruby wine in a crystal stem

the grass will grow, greenest in July
when the monsoons flourish
and the dry creeks spill their banks

hummingbirds will flock to the vine
driving their tiny drill bits down
the narrow bell to cull the nectar cache

children will rescue us from cynicism
inspire better versions of our ordinary selves
hold the mirror before us with expectant eyes

life and death and life will persist,
lovers will ignite, weather storms, forgive,
learn to trust, fall and rise again and yet again

Grace

all I know of earthly purpose
is about connection to life, human,
animal, plant, grounded in reverence

reaching for a handful of fertile earth
exhilarated by the spectacle of dawn
believing in beauty even when unseen

open to luminous revelation
filled with anticipation of spring's miracle
to follow the bitter blast of winter

living with the breath of hope
astonished by the drama of shadow and light
and the buoyancy of shared intentions

no settling of dust into the crevices
or under my feet — the path to be walked
whether in the trough or on the peak

love lavished like thick butter
on warm bread, an unbroken promise
that reminds me who I am.

Serenity

I yearn for many things
I don't really want —

for my youth which would frighten me
to stone should it return;

ambition, charged with self-belief
and achievement, but which now seems
a desperate attempt to avoid mirrors.

freedom, whose illusions once felt like
iron bands that cut my wrists.

now that autonomy is complete
I yearn for the boundaries of collaboration
and dialogue.

it is the yearning that renews my spirit,
my journey down rivers of small returns

when serenity seems preferable
to accomplishment.

The Poetry of Chaos

Wind rattles the trees, the sea grasses
bent low and sorrowful, while overhead
birds catch the draft balanced on the pinnacle,
moving neither forward or back on the current.

This is not the life I dreamed, this chaos
that somewhat resembles order, this flimsy life raft
adrift on a thrusting sea, lifted and dropped
amidst the detritus and dross.

I was enticed aboard, with the belief of a convert,
that I could captain this dismal, leaking craft,
pilot down my designated channels, avoid
the storms that befall the timid explorer.

I lean forward, eager to wash up on the shore,
amidst broken shells and mounds of kelp
where nourishment awaits, where wreckage
is an asset, and poems whisper on the wind.

Choices

So much depends
on a choice, a decision
to hear the voice
of the unlikely,
even the impossible,
that tells you to fly
anyway.

So much depends
on the *in spite of*
that becomes
the *because of*
where there is no
good reason
to keep going

and you do it
anyway.

Must Love Books

She made a list of attributes
required of any man
who would be invited in.

First was *must love books*
then a list of other *musts,*
a job, an education, a sense
of humor, but when it
came right down to it,

everything else could be dismissed
for only the first was important.

Perception

I am of the sky
floating in the hollow belly
of a meandering cloud

below lie lavender silhouettes
of mountain peaks, still bearing
chronicles of cliff dwellers,

their hearts exposed, revealing
how their shelters ground from the stones
provided everything needed

there the long, shadowy branches
of primordial trees and rocks
carry the knife-edged memory

of dark-eyed children running, women
sighing as fire, wind and dust
scattered their traces to the moonlight

from here I can name my ancients
earth, rain, sun, stars, grace
from the gods to thrive

and read the history of man
pressed into the chalky ground,
where wisdom was lost to greed

Fear of Crying

It can begin anywhere.
            I'm never prepared.

Then suddenly, there I am,
            again riding the tumult,
                        hands shaking, mouth dry,

quivering at the top
            of the diving platform

knowing I will do
            what is expected
                        of one who stands there,
as always I do.

Though I am deathly
            afraid of the plunge
                        all I can do is to

                                    launch into the air
to break the surface
            of what looks like
                        a deep aqua pool

but as I near the bottom I see
            that it is just a trifling
                        puddle of tears.

White Spaces

it's what isn't said,
isn't seen,
what remains idle,
disregarded,
dormant...

ah, therein
is the wealth
of what might have been,
words of healing,
connections made,
songs of hope sung,

lovers too long silent,
the time unrecoverable.

Daily Gift

in the sweet morning light
long silver-tipped grass
sweeps the meadow in cadence

with the vigorous breeze.
the fertile grazing ground vibrates,
sun diamonds shout for attention,

and I am beguiled once more
by the brilliance of this place,
this healing space that has embraced me

with its rough and dry dignity,
its evermore-ness, the luminosity
mysterious and curative, like a psalm,

in spite of everything.

Sunday Morning in San Francisco

Mist of rain, fog, of course, and yet a sweet
and favorite memory, especially alluring
because I had run away.

Leaving the hotel, wrapped in fleece,
feet in warm dry boots,
I was buoyant with expectation.

In the distance, a doleful foghorn bayed
its two cheerless notes, always the same,
warning of dangers which so excited me.

A corner coffee shop poured out its scent
onto the street, mingling with the musty smell
of fog, quickly drawing me in.

The foam cup warmed my hands
as I left the shop, headed down the hill,
to my temptress, a book store.

So early, almost empty, I moved inside the shop,
touching the bright covers as I browsed each table
piled high with someone's dreams.

Chopin softly embraced the morning quiet.
Perfect, I thought for the soundtrack of my escape.
I could merge myself between the pages and stay lost

in a picture-rich coffee table book
where I could explore in private the places
where I will go when I run away the next time,

as surely I will.

Vita Brevis

all the more reason
to cling
to the barest scrap
of love
however unlikely
or undeserved
to disturb
sacred beliefs
unravel
cherished convictions
examine
established truth
be done
with useless
arguments

Homecoming

Here, a gathering of familiar strangers pass
through the mirrors of their own disparate
expectations of family.

Their faces you could trace
with your fingers in the air, their laughter
like chords of a remembered song,

their tears never quite revealing the discordant
notes they hear, only that it is not the song
their hearts require.

We read into each other's hieroglyphs
stories of our own deficiencies,
bridges not quite meeting a faraway shore

where the bitter and the benevolent live together
in nominal peace, the truth and its absence
seeming equally credible.

Here is where the book falls open to the place
we always return as a reminder of what binds us
and what draws us apart.

What Lasts

Unwrapping ornaments made of tightly woven memories
with bits of gold foil and tinsels that fall out each year,
hanging lights that illuminate the sacred moments
of connection and separation, the coming closer
to stand back and see the way we are.

How we stand in the kitchen because it is safe,
filled with scents that soothe the spirit so that
no careless words can break the festive mood,
pushing through the parts that seem like chores
to sit by the fire, breathing renewed warmth.

Songs to be sung, that made us who we are
and draw us into the picture we most love,
traditions and old jokes, familiar teasing among
siblings, who only remember the times before
we became many families, holding the string
of the kite that flew away.

Thanksgiving

The day is full, food and laughter,
music and games, richly laden tables
and flowing wine.

Before the day is gone, blessings
retired to the back of mind,
look around the room.

It is in the faces you see, the hands
you grasp in love, that bliss resides.
This is what you are seeking.

Touch tenderly those who gather
this day, remind yourself that it is all
you need — you are rich

beyond your dreams.

Bethlehem of My Heart

I am ready now
for the birth of hope,
the advent of trust,
heart poised to welcome
the faint music of angels.

Here the light of a star
shines on my persistent
struggle to exult in the now,
savoring the silken wrap
of love — my daily miracle.

I am ready now
to receive grace,
the spring in the desert,
the promise of a song sung
for as long as breath remains.

HOME

....

A Single Moment

In and out of the sunlight,
darting between familiar shadows,
patches of lucidity amidst the fog,
you search for connections and meanings
to understand what was effortless
just yesterday, but which now is gone.

I want to help you, fix you, hate you,
I want to scream, to laugh, to fall apart.
I long to be indifferent –
but I am too accustomed to loving you
to change now, the line between where you end
and I begin blurred like a garden of wildflowers.

I wish to be larger than this *mishap*,
this mystery that doctors only describe
in the vaguest terms, while our specifics
become memories that fade and falter,
your sweetness and submission exasperating
when I need a wall to push against.

My discontent feels gritty in my mouth
like pearls I have ground with my teeth.
I learn to avoid the fruit that will not ripen
and the metaphors without meaning.
I ride the back of the wind as far as I can go
in a single moment, for that is all there is.

Acceptance

it's music I didn't know
I knew until, one day,
I find myself singing
a song of surrender,
while pushing
a wheelbarrow
full of rocks
uphill.

Opening

but one day you just know...
that the struggle must end,

that the time for sadness is past
and the grieving stranger, no longer needed,
has gone for good;

that the sweet music you hear
is the rhythm of your hopeful heart
laden with gifts of nourishment,

a lavish feast for your hunger,
a warm cup for your deepest thirst
that you will not turn from, but embrace;

that you have come at last, searching
for yourself, clothed in grace,
to offer only love.

On the Edge

I wake and notice the house is on fire
yet I stare blankly into the morning;
I could douse the flames with a flood

of tears, and for a moment I am glad
not to have wasted them on lost love
or broken promises.

The changing colors of the dawn,
now muted and dull, draw my vision
out of focus and I sink deep into the gray,

the dark empty, where I disappear
in the mirror, only the outline of who
I used to be clear. I lean into the comfort

of melancholy, where everything makes sense,
nothing is about me and lonely is a warm
place, sustainable and friendly.

My hair needs brushing, the house still burns,
but it suddenly becomes important
to win at solitaire.

The Healing Desert

Come, I will take you to a secret place
in a dry land, an alluvial meadow
where the winds blowing down from
the mountains will find you,
bend into your fragile heart
and wait, wait to discover
where your deepest
wounds reside.

Like water finds its place
where there is a niche
to fill, the dry air will enfold you
as an embrace, in a moment
of grace, and spring will birth
a carpet of flowers, releasing you
from generations of pain
that you no longer own.

In the ancient valleys and barren slopes
where you have nothing but stones
from the river of loss, the sweetness of time
teaches patience; we forgive each other everything,
even the unforgivable, just to be sure
there is nothing left to hurt us,
nothing to separate us from our truth.

Threadbare

The fabric
is worn sheer,
fragile from pulling threads
to mend the fissures
of loss and grief,
unraveled in places,
worn through from stroking
wounds of disengagement,
sacred connections lost
to tangled neurons.

Still, the cloth I pull around
my empty shoulders
is strong for the task
and light enough to rise
with me in the morning,
with stubborn tenacity
to stand, alone when I must,
and find grace in the patched
and tattered garment of love
I wear to cover
us both.

What Love Is

Poets, when you write of love
don't speak of entwined hearts and eyes
locked in unflinching adoration.

Love is a sharp-edged, jagged
dead weight of a verb played out
on a moonscape of time.

No passive expressions of ardor;
words are no proof of affection
but frail surrogates for intimacy.

Dig for treasures in the dust
if you must, but rocks are brittle
and dry, they pinch the flesh,

piercing the thin skin of truth
and leave angry sores that linger
to surface in unexpected rhythms.

Do not attempt love expecting
the easy caress of a summer night
but the howling shriek of winter's blast

that pounds your fragile love
into the frozen ground, to wait
until spring's warmth calls it to emerge.

Dare to love because only its absence
would surely cause more pain, and you know
you are bound like wings of the same bird.

Love only if you have no choice,
no voice, but cannot breathe
without your other self.

The Icarus Parable

Oh, these fine combustible chambers
of ourselves, blissfully embraced and explored,
the incomparable wonder at the way
each of us has remained whole
while absorbed into the other.

The question always was: how close
to the sun could we fly? how much grace
could we attract and hold our poise?
It is as if something in our core
expected our wax wings to melt when
we reached our azimuth, our true north.

The End of the Feast

The knowledge burst upon me
like a startled covey of quail
taking sudden panicked flight,
lightning writ across the sky
flashing what should have been obvious,
that I must loosen my grip
on the smoke I hold
in my hand.

That which cannot be changed
must be transformed into something
survivable; I who could mend anything,
change the course of tides, move planets —
it shouldn't be so difficult to salvage
hope, to remember why we live,
this is such a small thing,
an easy fix.

I learned to sing my grief
and breathe through the sadness
of loss, to ask for smaller joys
and find nuggets of pleasure
in our rituals, your warm hand once
the same as mine, the unity
that nothing could shatter,
a feast forever.

Even the altering wind
would hold us close in shelter
but now, here, facing the storm
that found our breach, now,

here is the shadow of a shadow
and we reach for each other
with cold hands, our valuables
locked forever in an empty safe.

Promise

whisper my name in the blue-gray dawn
when light begins to seep up from the ground,
call for me when the silken shadows of afternoon
drop soft on the hills, their velvet folds aglow.

beckon with just a gesture when the sun slips
low and the stars ascend in the black satin sky
with just a breath or a silent wish, reach out
to touch my waiting hand, my warm cheek.

even when, my name long forgotten, you know
my touch, scent of my skin, sound of my smile,
the memories may be broken, but not the sanctuary
of our union, born in intimacy, forged in grief.

call me to sit beside you and turn the pages
of the story of our life, the pictures of happy people
whose faces you don't recall, the places you think
you have never been, though you smile back at me.

summon me to stay near by, as always I will,
to play your favorite Beethoven and Brahms
and remind you of the mystical days we held
so dear, when fortune smiled at our courage.

Mirage

In my dream
I am calling you, calling you
back from a place the color
of solitude, only your outline
visible through dusty curtains.

Music plays somewhere,
a concerto you love,
the Emperor,
and I think you will hear
and follow the sound
but you don't.

It's me, I call, remember me?
You don't.

I notice parts of you,
like misty filaments,
blowing away in
a sudden violent gust
silhouetted in starlight,
and my throat strains,
screaming now, to stop.

You don't.

The wanting is not enough,
nor the hunger that never ends;
my mistake for believing
in hope as a strategy.
But then, I have always thought
I had magical powers.

You never did.

Disclaimer

I don't want your love.
it is far too much trouble
and I am long gone.

I just want quiet —
peace without expectation;
alone I'm enough.

walk in a light breeze,
feed strawberries to the dogs,
laugh through caustic tears.

sing songs in the wind,
wear a silken gown to bed,
love my aging bones.

dance to loud music,
drink wine till I am happy,
pretend nothing hurts.

Pain

Don't touch my pain;
don't speak of it in whispers.

You are not granted rights to act
as if you know.

Don't make me tea,
inquire if I am cold
or bring me the paper.

When I am ready to open
to you a bit the light
will slip under the door

and I will invite you
for a moment, a moment

but you must know when
it is time to leave.

You can't take my pain
when you go, but you can
leave a space in which to return.

Camouflage

Like birds the color of dirt and leaves,
I long to merge with my surroundings,
become a mist that seeps silently into cracks
and crannies, undetectable, weaving a web
of feathers and dust to encircle my tender organs.

I hug the ground, rebuffing hawk and kestrel,
who flamboyantly pierce the sky
while quail and wren occupy their familiar terrain,
ordinary, common, nearly invisible,
under a low and brittle thicket.

I want a cloak, a mythical disguise,
to hide, to heal, to regain my identity,
to be a shy Elegant Trogon or Pileated Woodpecker,
hiding among shadowed branches to camouflage
their flashy plumage and hide their vulnerable bones.

I yearn to be a flickering light in a firefly forest,
ignored and concealed, soothing my injured wings,
alone in a cedar, where the moon splits the darkness quietly,
and a great horned owl turns his eyes to me
with indulgence.

What I still want

it will have to be a long walk
for the tears to dry and leave
their salt tracks on my face,
for my anger to exhaust its heat
in surrender

past dry creeks, white sycamores
and deadfallen oaks
where now small creatures
draw their sustenance
from decay,

past the sun's long shadow
in that moment before it ends,
that shimmering instant when
everything smolders in the breathless
angle of completion.

I will walk until yesterday,
before life unraveled,
wanting the impossible —
why not? I ask, it's what
I always wanted.

Lament for Haiti

the ground twists
sickeningly
with timeless equanimity,
a natural occurrence
in the planetary construct,
unconcerned
that we will not be able
to comprehend, the devastation
too complete.

the family of earth weeps
that all has been taken
from those with nothing,
to heap upon the afflicted
a new portion of torment
leaving an ocean of primal grief
to lap at a crumbled shore
as though nothing had changed,

don't look away —
stare into the fractured night
where even the stones cry out,
heartbroken
watch in silent disbelief,
as if the earth had disowned
a whole people
where forever only suffering
will survive.

don't turn away —
look, you recognize them,
they are us, they are us.

Never Satisfied

When it was mid summer and relentless
sun filled every corner, the slow afternoons
ablaze with heat-induced lethargy,

my mother yearned for the feel
of a thick warm sweater and cold mornings,
coffee by the fireplace, feet clad in wool.

When it was dead of winter, barren and brittle
with a fretwork of low shadows on the snow
she could only shiver and talk of summer's glory.

In the dry season, where was the rain?
When it poured, would it ever stop?
And the discontented hours grew to years.

No wonder I was afraid when she was happy,
strangely at ease when all hell broke loose
and never quite content in the moment.

Over

Their eye contact is infrequent
and without light, lips dry
and barely parted
when they speak
to each other's back.

He made her laugh;
she ignited a warmth
he didn't know he had
but now never showed.
She hadn't laughed in months.

Their holiday letters
recount their son's achievements,
the vacation in Cancun
but no mention of the chasm
that had called them to the edge

and flayed their bodies with
searing indifference, passion
long-forgotten or destroyed
by cadaverous apathy
and the miasma of disappointment.

They agreed it was over
but since neither could picture
the afterlife of a marriage
they donned costumes and masks,
played out the familiarity
of endurance,

neither wanting to be the first to go.

Quiet Rage

The steel blue anger always worked before
to bring me back, focus the animal
energy that terrified and savaged me,
my dependable companion, thick with reason,
lifting the film of irrational optimism from my eyes
to remind that anger is the only emotion
I trust.

Here is the anger that will not be mollified,
cannot be turned to music or metaphors,
the hopeless surrendering with slumped shoulders,
the voice quiet and the body turned concave
to fight off attempts to believe in counterfeit
happiness again.

I am defenseless, shadowy
in the mirror, no return from the dark path
that leaches my spirit, fills my throat
with razors, spiraling my voice
down the drain clockwise, to pool
with the deranged.

Survival

My mother never forgave
my father for getting sick
so she burned down the marriage
with them both still in it,
fanning the flames
with Salome's veils soaked
in bourbon, dancing most nights
till she fell in a stupor
to the floor.

We were co-conspirators
of the family holocaust,
keepers of the tribal secrets,
the blindfold of silence
covering our eyes, denial
playing its siren's song.
There were no answers
because no one knew
what questions to ask.

Alone together, each filled
a personal sack of melancholy
hiding the truth that all knew
but could not speak.
My secret was that joy was possible
if I could just survive childhood.

The Way They Were

The sepia-toned honeymoon photo,
1936, strolling Chicago's Michigan Avenue,
arm in arm, the only evidence I have that they loved
each other once — that, and my existence.

They gaze at each other with playful affection
and an intimacy dwindled to indifference
by the time I arrived on the scene.

They survived in parallel loneliness,
rendered emotionally impotent, he, by his disease,
she by dry martinis, using their disappointment to fix

each other in place, I the specimen into which
they stuck their pins of longing, who waited to escape
into the first proposal of marriage
no matter how doomed.

Vespers

Stand here with me, on the edge of dusk,
while the descending sun, trailing it's pale orange slip
across a lilac sky, reluctantly surrenders the day.

Stand and watch the dark creep forward
and feel the resolute air as birds find sheltering limbs,
their songs growing faint in the night breeze.

Feel the quiet twilight music lay upon your weariness,
cool as the throat of a lily, calm as a baby's sigh.
let the night curve into your arms, your spine,

your face, like the dropping of a silken scarf
that strokes it's gentle caress over your regret.
In this sacred moment of relinquishment
drink in the sweet holy hush.

HEALING

....

Garden Dream

It's always the same...
dawn slips under the door, I enter a garden
exotic and profuse, blossoms resembling rare gems
in wild array, a pond of silver minnows like tears of rain,
and she is there, bent over the lavender, star flower
and amaranth, a straw hat covering her wispy hair.
She smiles, and the barest nod invites me closer,
to breathe the lilies and hyacinth,
the sweetness of basil and rosemary.

I perceive her as a treasure in my life that somehow
I have forgotten — I know her, yet I do not. Her eyes
are sorrow reflected in a lake, her mouth a silent rose,
a familiar anguish in the curve of her spine.
My hand reaches out to touch the cupped petals,
the magenta, metallic green, the white and butter gold.
In the drape of her skirt she gathers a fragrant bouquet,
turns slowly, offers it to me, and I realize that
I am in *her* dream.

Escape

The breath was gone from those days —
I wore my mornings loosely
filling the hours with a million small demands
for chunks of my heart,
my songs unsung.

Afternoons when the sun flared gold
I stared into small lit faces
and tried to imagine with what birds
they would fly away
to sing their songs.

I gave away my songs for illusions,
traded my barely-formed image in the mirror
for someone else's picture of me
and, smiling, disappeared
into the mist.

But oh, the nights, when the swirling wind swept in,
disposing of my glassy, spider-web dreams
and unsung songs, I recklessly let the dark take me
to the time before I crossed over
into acquiescence.

Butterfly Bush

Under a corrugated morning sky
purple spikes flutter to life.

They quiver on perfect silent wings
in an effortless jazz ballet,
kissing flower, branch and blossom.

It is all they do, the sacred mystery
of single purpose creatures,
faint brushstrokes on a summer canvas,

moving the air, transforming everything
into light, weightless and faultless.
They live in transparency, feed on fragrance.

I press myself inside their world,
to be lifted here and there by a mere breath,
to feel powerful with divine intention.

I want to live in a flower.

A Moment in Time

Could ever I have been so busy
that I missed the shadows on the hills
changing from brown to mauve to violet
in the impatient twilight?

Could I have found any single thing
more enchanting than a gaggle of birds
swarming the feeder to juggle
for their place amidst the seed?

How could anything satisfy as deeply
as the gentle curves of life that now bend
around this home in the golden hills

where the sun kisses the tops of the grasses
and wind propels itself exuberantly through
the doors of my heart, tossing leaves for fun?

What could have been more compelling
than sitting still before the darkened window
where a ribbon of orange, with a firm
brush stroke, was painting morning?

The steep slope of time is mostly behind me —
no need to pass quickly through the small songs.
I stand in the rests between the notes
to more clearly hear the harmonies.

Three a.m.

singing to myself
again, a tune
that will not quit

while dark sprites
arrange themselves
single file

to march goose-step
across the goose down
their droning

drowning out
the songs
in my head

Beach Birds

I have trekked to the gulf,
towel, book and cooler,
seeking immersion in
waves, wind, scorching
white sand and sea grass.

a dozen black terns peck
at a mass of kelp, finding treasure,
while I am immobilized
by the radiant warmth, beating surf,
I want to stay...stay here

drowsy in the heat, as
a stretch of brown pelicans
define the horizon,
stitching sea and sky together
over white-tipped water.

breakers reach the warm shallows,
slant their approach to the shore,
heaving the sandy bed in and out;
the air insistent, laying heavy on the skin,
like a tight glove, while sandpipers dart

and overhead gulls plunge and wheel,
hovering on the currents, loudly
claiming their scavenger rights
to the debris of a thousand tides
that neither begin nor end here.

Coyote at Dawn

he stands
in a cold morning rain,
wind-ruffled coat blending
with mottled grasses,
mesquite and greasewood,
straight-stretched hunter's legs
looking swift even while still,
through the dreary drizzle
his eyes fixed on me
in a golden blaze
of primeval wisdom
and wariness.

wild one, you live
the best you can,
just as I do.

Cycle

having let go
her brittle autumn glitter
the sycamore shivers
in a winter dress
white bones bleak
as a ribcage
waiting in the void
for the turned-in earth
to waken and dress itself
once more

Certain Beloved Graces

Why has this come as a surprise?
this body I have inhabited for seventy years —
surely someone else's masquerade costume
donned by mistake, cannot belong to me,
here where the light is all wrong, shadows emerge.

I fear, with a shock of hubris, that I do not know
how to grow old without giving up everything
that defines me, or know why I still feel
like the least mature person I know,
requiring drama and angst to thrive,

still want what lies just outside my vision
still caught between compulsions
and commitments. I wear this age like a thin robe
that hangs on back of the bathroom door
to wear only when I'm alone.

The thing is, I don't remember young
unless it was that time when I was happily swollen
with babies, filled with anxiety, an occupied country
trying to decide if I was the warden
or the prisoner seeking amnesty.

Yet, here I am with all my passions intact
to sing, to write, to be an outrageous *older woman,*
the years conceded like the sound of falling snow
left with little yet to decide and granted
certain beloved graces.

Graffiti

finding a voice for words scorched
across my heart like a burning torch,
places where I have not left the door ajar
nor given expression to fear and hunger

finding courage to call things
by their right names, knowing
I am capable of feelings on feelings
love upon anger upon love

finding peace in the experience
of mystery, knowing all is at risk
while letting go to be consumed
by the fire, without regret

Hummingbird

He flew by mistake
into the open garage door,
drawn inward toward a window
he must have expected led to freedom.

Wings beat a panicked throbbing,
rising and falling against the glass
as I gently cupped my hand beneath his tiny body
and he collapsed into my palm.

Gasping at the incredible weight of nothingness
that could produce such energy, I lifted my hand
to the sky to return this impossible creature
to the miniature world he owns,
joy rising.

If there is heaven…

If there is heaven somewhere besides here
there will be a lapis sky with towering clouds,
mountain peaks, great books and good cheer,

the small black dog who broke my heart by dying,
deer to silently return my gaze and hawks
creasing the sky with seamless flying

there will be friends ready to laugh awhile
and we will speak our truth when it feels right
and lie a little if it makes a loved one smile.

No one will be embarrassed to get up and dance,
wine will flow, succulent food without guilt,
candles, soft breezes and always a little romance.

The Bach Double Concerto will soar when day is gone
Natalie Dessay will sing Traviata to a dark sky,
and Itzhak will play The Lark Ascending at dawn.

Great New Orleans jazz is always flowing
because, please understand, if the music isn't good
I'm just not going.

Fresh Flowers

Two bunches of alstroemeria
from the supermarket,
deep crimson and pink/white,
with speckled throats thickly
clustered in a round cobalt vase,
catch the glint of the sun,
and burnish an arc
across the dining room table.

Each time I pass I inhale
their delicate splendor and smile.
It doesn't take much to make me happy.

Gazebo

On a flawless summer afternoon,
she sits apart by the spangled sea,
within a trellis of random branches.
Gulls perforate the air, burnished
in the sun, blurred in their freefall
against the sheer cobalt sky.

White linen shirt, air-billowed
skirt, bare brown feet, wisps
of russet hair ruffled by the spindrift,
cool on her face, she leans into the lattice
and breathes the primal ocean scent,
feeling gathered in by the insistent surf.

On her lap a book with a red cover,
her finger idly tracing the title.
Here a picture so complete in detail
and composition no one will dare
to enter the frame and so she remains
perfectly alone.

Spanish Night

With what words to describe that night?
Silence the better choice when speechless with pleasure,
just to hold the memory against my heart...
      an evening in May, a quiet cantina,
            sitting melancholy with loss.

A single guitarist exhaled Granados with lonely fingers,
his dark eyes deep with recall, each string stroked
as if a woman, under an arched moon,
      remembered the way his hands felt
            but could not remember to breathe.

With what words did his melodies speak?
lovers urging toward a darkened villa, their passion lighting
the grey shadows, a slow embrace with tender intent,
      scent of the trumpet vine, brushed
            with a fragrant breeze from the sea.

I embraced the glass, tequila's golden warmth,
knowing the moment would be a touchstone,
a reminder that dreams live quietly, making room
      for quixotic fantasy, a mental escape
            when reality crowds out the wistful
              remembrance of that one night.

Still Perfect After All These Years

Full moon sometimes known as blue,
held above by the barest thread
of spider web silk
setting my window ablaze
with the hopeless perfection I so envy,
just as thin and beautiful as ever,
never less desirable, even in your
old age.

No one tires of looking at you,
though by now we should be jaded
with your predictable appearance,
mirrored on water, gleaming over
a field of snow, teetering on
a mountain edge; you make us breathless
each time just as the first.

No one cries "can't we have a newer moon?"
No one deplores your sameness
or wishes you just a bit larger or smaller;
you have not become irrelevant to our lives
just because we know you so well.
No one needs more than one moon,
do they?

January Light

creaking winter,
thin, breakable,
angled at a deep slant,
you come across my doorstep,
late and lazy, the dark resisting
your glow, fragile, with clear
intention not to linger
at the end of the day

so soon you compel the spring
and summer to work round
the planetary calendar
while you barely break a sweat
to light the earth with porcelain
mornings and the brief passing
of twilight

Monsoon Colors

I live on a red dirt road
which today the monsoon rain
has made slick as an oil spill;

the stunning storms also bring clouds
like a blinding avalanche in the sky,
and turn the golden grasses to green

of too many shades to count, brilliant against
a cornflower blue sky. I am awash in color,
almost too sharp, so stunning my eyes ache

with bliss, and I greedily claim this place as mine,
perilous as life is, grateful for delicious morsels
that quench a thirsty heart with grace.

There Will Be Singing

Where the music plays
emptiness has no home.

It is my Sanctus, my Gloria,
like prayers pinned to a wall.

It is a Brahms symphony, a Mozart aria,
a Bach Mass that lifts me above

simple hearing to absorbing
the essence of creation, the light.

Though my existence feels slight
I am anchored in genius that never fails.

It is the *nevertheless* of hope
the sacred peril of daring

to rise, fall and rise again,
with the music, the deliberate

threshing of the significant
from the trivial, arms stretched out,

to feel the pulse in the air, thrumming
off the walls as I find my way home

by sonar ping so I can sing
from rim to rim, edge to edge,

relentlessly moving toward the sound
that immerses me, changes me,

rushes through me like a river on a mission
to transform my temporary wreckage.

Seasons

I revel in the teasing game the seasons play;
Each makes its alluring play for attention,
the competition requiring a display of excess.

Oh spring, you outdo them all each year, rewarding
our survival with longer days, clement breezes
and displays of unbridled fervor. Lambs are born,
birds return with a glint of red, a splash of yellow,
and even rocks seem to bloom from their mossy beds.

Summer makes noisy demands; we must be doing,
going, desperate to wring every minute of sunlight
from every perfect day, no time to savor, but hurry
to gather each pleasure, each fragrant flower
to press between the pages of time.

Autumn blushes against the sky in a rage of colors,
a gaudy showgirl, fickle and tumultuous.
Unexpected winds cut suddenly across the road,
scoop up clouds of red dust, and whip the tall grass,
while the days quickly change from hot to cold and back.

Fierce winter plays her hardest game, laughing
when children bless the snow and adults curse it.
Her frozen sky gives little back but a gray disregard.
She gives up slowly, her icy chill reluctant
to surrender to spring's charming temptation,

until finally, admitting defeat, she waves the white flag
and heads for a different hemisphere, where people tire
of fall's cacophony of color, and are ready to welcome
the gentle demise of the year, mantled in no color at all,
to rest for the duration.

Narcissist

Don't argue.
It is useless — you can't
win an argument with him.
The insidious way he wrecks
the people he says he loves,
the fault, the error,
mistake in judgment
never his, could not be,
begs you to be honest,
share your feelings,
the ones about how much
you admire him and are sorry
for the hurt you have caused
for so long.

Lethal to all who dare
confront the jovial demeanor,
the soft voice so empathic
hiding the subtle poison
of self-hate,
you will be his banner
which he will fly from
a high place to proclaim
how misunderstood
and ill-used he is,
his cardboard face smiling
that indulgent smile
and you will apologize
time and again
until one day

you reclaim your glass heart
so it cannot be broken again.

String Beans

When I was three
you made me sit with you on the floor
in that New Orleans narrow hallway
stringing beans into a kettle
because you panicked during storms.
Even now, when I eat them
I hear thunder.

Winter Nocturne

listen,
the song is different now,
time has slowed, indifferent,
creation's adagio, windy
and secret places shelter
small creatures from frozen rocks,
the hard ground disguised
in a white dress

the ribs of barren trees stark
against a dark sky, streaming
clouds of warning, a fading moon
sings of lacy branches
in silhouette, while an owl
recalls his hollow flute song,
mellifluous in the frigid air

What To Do About God

so, I spent more than half my life
in church, soaking up promises,
feeling calmed and elevated,
singing the exquisite gifts
of the masters, believing
in God

in the rituals of daily salvation
and yet, here I am today,
suspicious of anything *religious*,
heart-sore and doubting
anyone who says he speaks
for God

mine, yours, does it matter what we call it?
is religion just a powerful
marketing scheme to divide us
from one another so that we
are vulnerable to persuasion
that pays off men in power
and has nothing to do
with God?

the thing is, I know the Divine,
the spiritual essence of life,
truth a river of love, prayer the search
that makes me part of creation,
like music, my mountain, the wind,
and it has everything to do
with God

when I can't leave my window
because the world is being re-created
before my eyes, and my heart swells
at the sight of a baby's birth,
acts of kindness by strangers
and the generosity of friends,
finally, doubt gone, this is all
I need to know
about God

Why Women Need Women

A woman friend to a woman is more precious
than privilege, a kindred who knows my battles
with direction, the weight thing, the hormones
that will not behave in a reasonable manner,
the terrors and joys of birthing and raising
small life forms, who feeds and clothes
her tribe all while negotiating
for world peace and cleaning up
the environment.

Someone else who has walked a lonely path
when dialogue seems like a deep and tortuous river,
and you have no boat, but are willing to swim.
When the man you love beyond all reason
goes Neanderthal, just short
of dragging you by your hair,
and you wonder what evil genius invented
marriage, knowing you would do it all
again without a second thought.

There is no substitute for a woman who laughs
and cries with the same desperation,
for whom pretense is never accepted
and who lifts you up while showing you the mirror.
She knows when to fight and when to quit
and why you sometimes prefer a lie to the truth.
No one else understands the effort it takes
for you to breathe life deeply, and offers you
the sweetness of never having to explain.

Too Soon

Where are the children who burst upon
the stream behind the house,
into the woods deep with fallen leaves,
their faces alive with delight, stippled
with sunlight and beaded creek water?

Where are the children whose bones we bore
under our hearts, who listened to our stories
of fairies and magic spells, over and over,
holding their breath with suspended belief,
their wide eyes intense?

Does not the child still need the mystery,
to ride the wind's back, the innocence
of learning the simple path of childhood,
the place where, at the right moment, truth
is peeled back one thin layer at a time?

Let their questions be of the sun, the grass,
how high the sky, what is the taste of green,
why can't I fly? what will I be when I grow up?
not like an ocean tide, but the flow of a river
that lifts them up when they are ready.

There is time to be old, so soon, so soon.
Rock the babes in a soft crescent moon
where they are nourished with plentiful love
and slow to taste the whole of life before
they have rolled in the sweet grass of youth.

Voices

Because someone must speak
for those who have not found their voices.

Because some echo in the silence, unobtrusive
as a cold desert night, alone in their affliction.

Because my churning passion is not yours
though I am convinced of its worth,

I need to hear your voice, vibrant
with the alarm you hear in your darkness.

Because you may hate what I honor
and your fervor drive me mad,

because smoke and angels and oblivion
are all figments of our own creation,

because childhood, love, death, pain
joy and fear are our universal bonds,

I need to hear your raucous voice, though it
breaks through my cherished convictions and rips

apart my own prejudice and terror,
your face in the mirror alarmingly like mine.

Because we cannot exist as one reflection,
one ambition, one monolith of similarity...

because we would die of our sameness
disappearing into the silence of solitary thought.

Winter Night

Snow-sugared branches glow
in the fading light, the cold crackling
the windows with fingers of frost.

A rare night at home together..
after dinner we agree, no TV,
and I select soft guitar adagios.

I pour a favorite red, light musky-
scented candles, silently admire the lines
in your strong face that I so love.

You gather me from random thoughts,
to where you have carefully laid the fire
and I smile, knowing

I am next.

Endings

Like the slithery transition between
sleep and waking, a year begins to slip
into history, taking with it those capricious
moments when everything was possible.

Endings bring sadness, no more chances
to shape events, pull from the distractions
in my head the jagged start-stop regret
of best intentions.

Leaves whirl from my tree of hope,
gather on the damp ground, slowly
decaying into new life, but forever lost
to my mania for fixing what went wrong

with this year's plan — going for the dreams
and passions that I always knew would not
survive loneliness or bring me comfort. I see them
dangling at my window, and once again

I believe in beginnings.

8334261R0

Made in the USA
Charleston, SC
30 May 2011